Deserving is Spiritual

Affirmational Journey to Inner Healing

T. AN

Copyright © 2023 by T. AN

All rights reserved. No part of this publication may be reproduced, stored or transmitted in any form or by any means, electronic, mechanical, photocopying, recording, scanning, or otherwise without written permission from the publisher. It is illegal to copy this book, post it to a website, or distribute it by any other means without permission.

First edition

This book was professionally typeset on Reedsy.

Contents

Preface	vii
DAY 1	1
Reflection	2
DAY 2	3
Reflection	4
DAY 3	5
Reflection	6
DAY 4	7
Reflection	8
DAY 5	9
Reflection	10
DAY 6	11
Reflection	12
DAY 7	13
Reflection	14
DAY 8	15
Reflection	16
DAY 9	17
Reflection	18
DAY 10	19
Reflection	20
DAY 11	21
Reflection	22

DAY 12	23
Reflection	24
DAY 13	25
Reflection	26
DAY 14	27
Reflection	28
DAY 15	29
Reflection	30
DAY 16	31
Reflection	32
DAY 17	33
Reflection	34
DAY 18	35
Reflection	36
DAY 19	37
Reflection	38
DAY 20	39
Reflection	40
DAY 21	41
Reflection	42
DAY 22	43
Reflection	44
DAY 23	45
Reflection	46
DAY 24	47
Reflection	48
DAY 25	49
Reflection	50
DAY 26	51
Reflection	52
DAY 27	53

Reflection	54
DAY 28	55
Reflection	56
DAY 29	57
Reflection	58
DAY 30	59
Reflection	60
About the Author	61

Preface

This piece celebrates embracing love for everything I was told I didn't deserve. My upbringing made it challenging to be my true free-spirited self and fully articulate my identity. I lost sight of myself in that process. The potency of our thoughts and words often goes unnoticed. I trust this book will guide you to recognize the spiritual essence of deservingness. Over thirty days, may these pages sow seeds in your mind, affirming that deservingness is your innate birthright.

—T. AN

DAY 1

I Deserve…

freedom, whatever that may look like for me. I won't allow anyone to impose their ideas of freedom upon me. I will define my own framework of freedom.

Reflection

DAY 2

I Deserve…

to wake up and set the intentions for my day. I will initiate my intentions and manifest them by harnessing the desired energy. I will master my day.

Reflection

DAY 3

I Deserve…

to know that I am prepared for this journey, encompassing every challenge. Hardships are transient; they neither endure nor shape my identity. Regardless, joy is inherently mine.

Reflection

DAY 4

I Deserve…

to be thankful. Thankfulness produces abundance. What am I thankful for?

Reflection

DAY 5

I Deserve…

to enjoy the present and not worry too much about the future. There are miracles found in the now.

Reflection

DAY 6

I Deserve…

to put myself first. My happiness, mental and emotional health, and overall well being come first.

Reflection

DAY 7

I Deserve...

to stand up for myself and not back down. What does standing up for myself look like?

Reflection

DAY 8

I Deserve…

to know that I am more than enough! I recognize the inherent value within myself.

Reflection

DAY 9

I Deserve…

good people; good people need good people. I will take the time to identify the good people in my life and reciprocate their kindness.

Reflection

DAY 10

I Deserve…

love and respect. I won't sacrifice one for the other.

Reflection

DAY 11

I Deserve…

to shed layers of myself. I give myself permission to grow and transform.; only my permission matters. What ideas do I have for growth?

Reflection

DAY 12

I Deserve...

to protect my energy at all costs. What boundaries do I need to put in place?

Reflection

DAY 13

I Deserve...

peace. I can't put a price on peace. How do I define peace?

Reflection

DAY 14

I Deserve…

a love that will honor me. What is love? What is honor?

Reflection

DAY 15

I Deserve…

to do whatever makes my heart sing. What brings me happiness?

Reflection

DAY 16

I Deserve…

to walk away from what no longer serves me. What do I need to let go of?

Reflection

DAY 17

I Deserve…

to know it's okay to make mistakes. Learn, heal, grow.

Reflection

DAY 18

I Deserve…

to trust in love again. I will trust in love again and I will trust myself.

ps://translate.goog/

Reflection

DAY 19

I Deserve…

to know what I believe about myself is the catalyst for what I receive in life. What's my view of myself?

Reflection

DAY 20

I Deserve…

to trust myself. I will listen to that inner voice; it's there to protect and guide me.

Reflection

DAY 21

I Deserve...

care, tenderness, and all the pleasantries of life. How do I define enjoyment?

Reflection

DAY 22

I Deserve…

a life of luxury or simplicity; I decide the terms. What brings me pleasure?

Reflection

DAY 23

I Deserve…

to know it's okay to feel. It's a great sign that I'm still alive. What feelings can stay and what feelings need to go?

Reflection

DAY 24

I Deserve…

to know that I can have anything that I desire; the only limits are my thoughts and mindset. What do I desire?

Reflection

DAY 25

I Deserve…

to rest. I will take some time to rest and reset. What does rest look like for me?

Reflection

DAY 26

I Deserve...

to understand that recognizing what I deserve also means acknowledging what I don't deserve.

Reflection

DAY 27

I Deserve…

to know that any time is the perfect time to MANIFEST. What are my manifestation goals?

Reflection

DAY 28

I Deserve…

to choose MYSELF every time, repeatedly. What does choosing myself look like?

Reflection

DAY 29

I Deserve…

to know that my healing journey is personal. I don't need permission to heal.

Reflection

DAY 30

I Deserve...

to believe. Belief unlocks boundless potential. What would I do if unbelief wasn't standing in the way?

Reflection

About the Author

T. AN, MBA, is a multi-talented woman whose journey seamlessly intertwines technology, design, the arts, and mysticism. With a passion for innovation, she found her footing in the world of technology, where she delved into cutting-edge advancements and embraced the power of digital creativity.

Her artistic soul, however, led her to explore the intricate world of fashion design, where she masterfully combines her technological prowess with a keen eye for aesthetics. Beyond her technological and fashion endeavors, she's deeply rooted in the arts and creativity, drawing inspiration from diverse mediums. Her artistic expression serves as a canvas to explore societal narratives and personal experiences, advocating for representation and empowerment.

Additionally, her journey into mysticism has granted her a unique perspective on life, spirituality, and interconnectedness. She embraces ancient wisdom, integrating it into her creative process, fostering a harmonious blend of spirituality and innovation.

You can connect with me on:

www.tantheauthor.com

Made in the USA
Columbia, SC
15 October 2024